To

....

From

....

ISBN-10: 0615805906

www.susanfierrobaig.com

Printed by Createspace.com
www.createspace.com/3885121

Photography
Susan's YOUnique Photography, Mais Oui Photography,
Chelsea Carrizales Photography and Robert-James Baig

Photo Editing
Kimberly Metz Photography Studio
Pixy Prints Photography

Book Design
Charlotte Vogel

Dedicated to
Margarita Refugia Olivas, Susana R. Lopez Garcia,
Lucy, Jennie, Rosario,
Robert,
C., R., E., M., A., D., C., B., B., G., L., N., M., K. and B.

In memory of
Ruby Gonzales, Toni "Coco" Burnham and Maria "BooBoo" Estrada.

Inspired by a Facebook conversation with Amber Galbraith.

A Mother's Worth:
Celebrating Motherhood

The worth of a mother can't be calculated by examining her bank account.

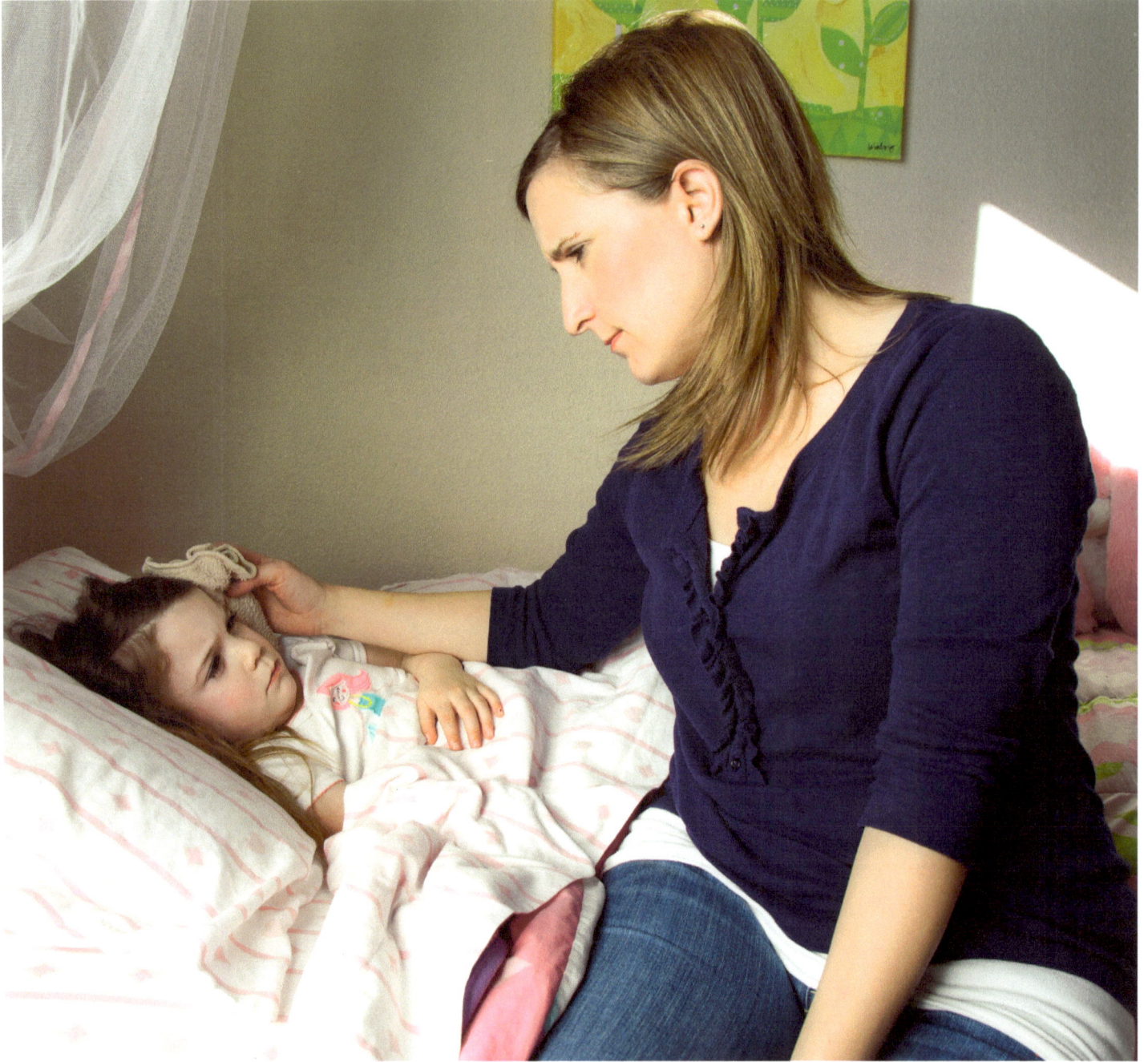

A mother performs many important jobs for her family that she is never paid for.
A mother is a nurse,

a teacher,

and a business manager.

A mother engineers monumental projects…

...and travels to far-away places.

Mothers are transportation specialists,

human relations experts,

counselors,

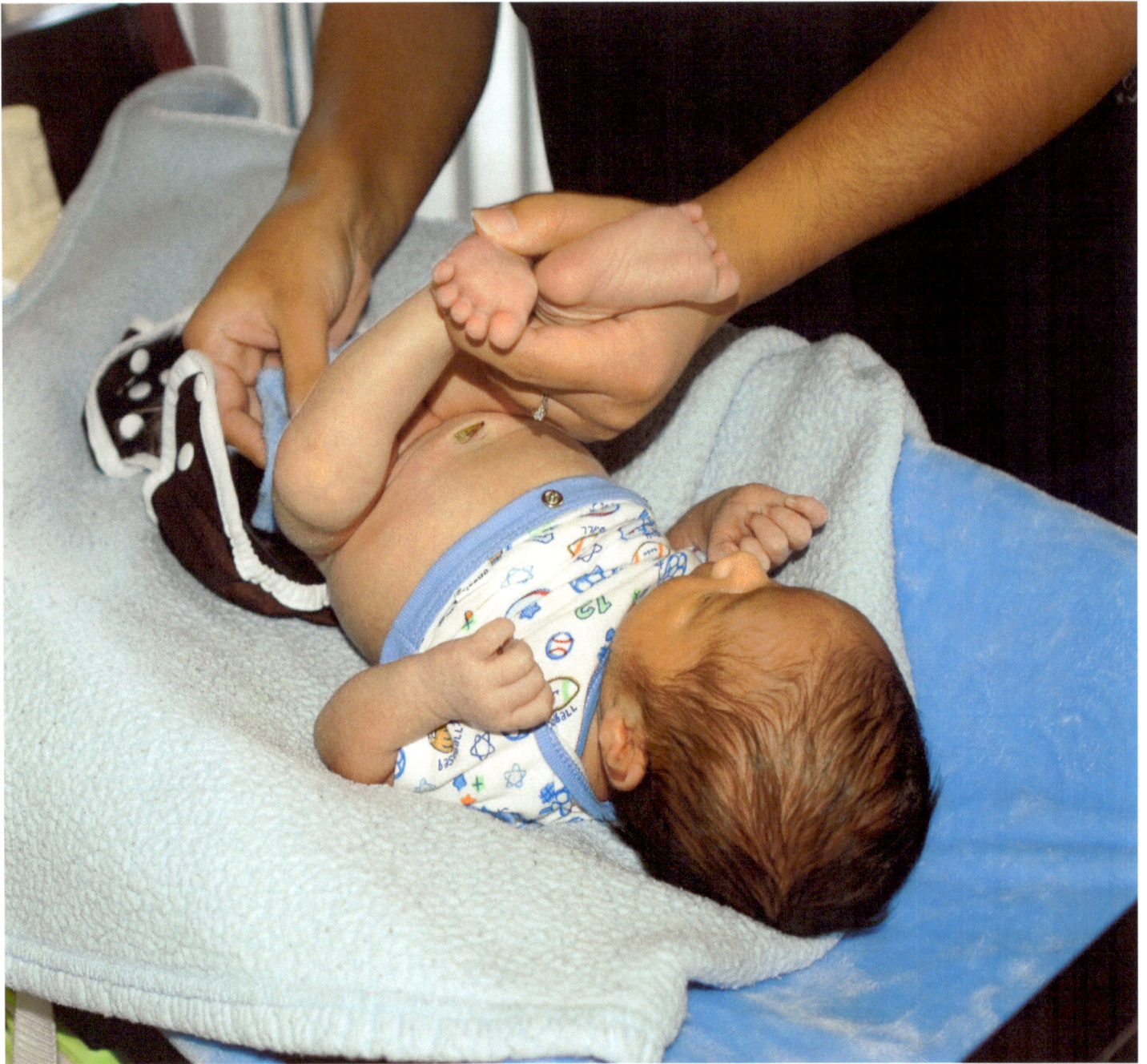

and sanitation waste operators.

Mothers are pastry chefs,

culinary artists,

and nutritionists.

A mother performs too many jobs to list them all.

Often she performs more than one job at the same time!

Mothers don't get paid for their hard work but they receive special honors. Mothers are rewarded with hearty hugs,

tender kisses,

And one~of~a~kind surprises.

Mothers are rewarded with adoring gazes,

heart-warming smiles,

priceless works of art,

and lavish gifts.

A mother is the queen of her kingdom.

Adhere photo here

The smiling faces of her children are a mother's greatest treasure.

Adhere photo here

A mother's worth is calculated by the deposits of love exchanged between her and her children – love makes her life very rich!

Adhere
photo
here

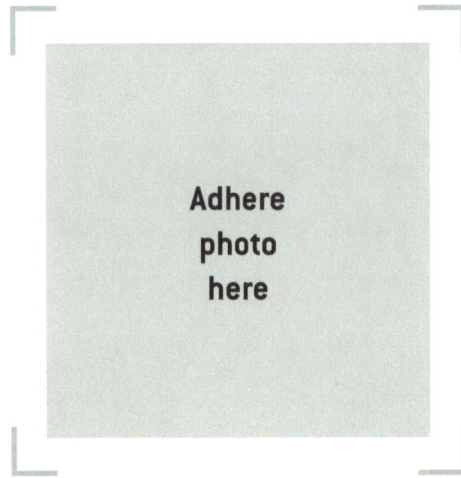

Mothers are priceless!

Order hard cover copies of this book:
www.amothersworth.net

Order soft cover copies of this book:
www.createspace.com/3885121

A Mother's Worth Facebook page:
facebook.com/AMothersWorth

Other books by the author:
Fast Adoption Fundraising
payhip.com/b/a5vR

Author's website:
www.susanfierrobaig.com

This book could not have been published without the financial contributions made via Kickstarter.com by Margarita Olivas, Jim & Jade Stacey, Eric Estrada, Danette Marsh, Benito & Diana Escobedo, Dorette English, Ralph & Sarah Rea, Janel Mirendah, Brittney Hales, Tony & Celia Lopez Sr., Dee Gordon, Virginia Ensign, Laurie Legore, Benjamin Hernandez, Tammy Christensen, Drew Allison, and Naoimi Cohen, as well as several unmentioned and anonymous donors.

SPECIAL MENTION
Susan Marsh, Alexandra Rutherford, Regina Villa and Sarah Price.

LINKS

Susan Fierro-Baig
www.facebook.com/SusansYouNiquePhotography

Kimberly Metz Photography Studio
www.kimberlymetz.com

Christina Bradberry
www.facebook.com/MaisOuiPhotography

Rachel Southmayd
www.facebook.com/PixyPrintsPhotography

Chelsea Carrizales
www.facebook.com/ChelseaCarrizalesPhotography

Charlotte Vogel
www.charlottevogel.com

SPECIAL THANKS
Most of the women involved in this book are military wives, stationed in 29 Palms, California. Many are members of the Church of Jesus Christ of Latter-day Saints. I am so grateful to all the families that opened their homes and posed for the photos. I saw the hand of God working as all those who participated in the modeling, photography, editing, and book design were brought serendipitously into the circle of this work.

Many thanks to my dear friend Jenny Hatch for her love and motherly example.

Thanks to Lily Miller of Blahblah Bebe Photography for her time and generosity.
www.facebook.com/pages/Blahblah-Bebe-Photography/218549001507675

PHOTO CREDITS
Susan Fierro-Baig
Cover; Inside cover 1, 3, 4, 5, 7;
Pgs. 3, 7, 8, 10, 12, 13, 16, 18, 19, 21, 24, 25

Christina Bradberry
Inside cover 2, 6, 8;
Pgs. 1, 2, 4, 9, 11, 14, 15, 20, 22, 23

Chelsea Carrizales
Pgs. 5, 6

Robert-James Baig
Pg. 17

www.ingramcontent.com/pod-product-compliance
Lightning Source LLC
Chambersburg PA
CBHW041221040426
42443CB00002B/46